THE LAWS OF PERSUASION

Persuasion Magazine

Persuasion Magazine

The Laws of Persuasion

Persuasion Magazine

CONTENTS

THE LAW OF DELIGHT
THE LAW OF DISTRACTION
THE LAW OF EASY
THE LAW OF EMPTINESS
THE LAW OF ENVY
THE LAW OF EXCITEMENT
THE LAW OF EXCLUSION
THE LAW OF EXPERTISE
THE LAW OF FAITH
THE LAW OF FANTASY
THE LAW OF FEAR
THE LAW OF FREE
THE LAW OF FREEDOM
THE LAW OF FRUSTRATION
THE LAW OF FULFILLMENT
THE LAW OF FUTURE
THE LAW OF GREED
THE LAW OF GROWTH
THE LAW OF GUILT
THE LAW OF HERO WORSHIP
THE LAW OF HOARDING
THE LAW OF HOPE
THE LAW OF IDENTITY
THE LAW OF IMMORTALITY
THE LAW OF INADEQUACY
THE LAW OF INSIDER STATUS
THE LAW OF INTRIGUE
THE LAW OF JEALOUSY
THE LAW OF LAZINESS
THE LAW OF LONELINESS
THE LAW OF LOSS
THE LAW OF LUST
THE LAW OF MAGIC
THE LAW OF MECHANISM
THE LAW OF MOTIVATION
THE LAW OF NARRATIVE
THE LAW OF NEW
THE LAW OF NORMALCY
THE LAW OF NOSTALGIA
THE LAW OF NOVELTY
THE LAW OF OBEDIENCE

THE LAW OF OBLIGATION

THE LAW OF OPTIMISM

THE LAW OF PANIC

THE LAW OF PARANOIA

THE LAW OF PERMISSION

THE LAW OF POSSIBILITY

THE LAW OF POWER

THE LAW OF PRIDE

THE LAW OF PROOF

THE LAW OF PUBLICITY

THE LAW OF RECOGNITION

THE LAW OF REDEMPTION

THE LAW OF REGRET

THE LAW OF REMEDY FOR DISCOURAGEMENT

THE LAW OF RESOLUTION

THE LAW OF REVENGE

THE LAW OF SAFE

THE LAW OF SATISFACTION

THE LAW OF SCARCITY

THE LAW OF SECRET KNOWLEDGE

THE LAW OF SELF-DOUBT

THE LAW OF SHAME

THE LAW OF SPECTACLE

THE LAW OF STATUS

THE LAW OF STICKING IT TO THE MAN

THE LAW OF SUPERIORITY

THE LAW OF SUPERSTITION

THE LAW OF SUSPICION

THE LAW OF THE ENEMY

THE LAW OF TRUST

THE LAW OF URGENCY

THE LAW OF VALIDATION

THE LAW OF VALUE

THE LAW OF VANITY

THE LAW OF VICTORY

THE LAW OF VIOLENCE

THE LAW OF VITALITY

INTRODUCTION

This slim handbook is designed to help sales professionals create advertising that sells. You will find over 100 emotional triggers in this book. Our premise is that people do not buy products – they buy the emotional triggers that are associated with those products. We live in a world that is essentially a 360° crafted narrative. We are all driven by emotions that have been embedded in the environment. We are all trying to satisfy the emotions that arise from that programming. None of us are immune to it.

Advertising is so sophisticated it drives our inner psychology. The challenge today is to understand the hidden drivers of our customers' lives and to satisfy them. To use this book you simply need to ask the same question over and over again. What are the emotional triggers in my customer? You see your product does not create the emotion. Your job is to position your product and your message so that it satisfies the emotions that are already in the customer. This is a profound understanding of modern commerce. We are all operating on a stimulus and response basis. Your advertising is the stimulus, and your desired response is the customer's money. You can close the loop by creating advertising that speaks directly to the emotions in your prospect.

Emotional triggers are the precursor to copywriting. One of the reasons people have a hard time writing words is they don't have a target in mind. We start with the customer's emotions. One of the great insights into advertising is that emotions are not in the product. They are in the customer. All good advertising does is associate the emotions that are already in the customer to the product being sold.

This is a short book. It is meant to be used as a tool. Carry it with you. You can open to any page, read the bullet points for an emotional trigger and then you'll see the same question over and over again throughout this document:

How can you associate your product with the emotional trigger of X in your customer?

This approach might take some getting used to and that is understandable. That's why we have a free spreadsheet you can download at our website. Here is the link: https://substack.com/@persuasionmagazine .

Before you start writing paragraphs of copy take the time to fill out the spreadsheet and identify multiple emotional triggers. You will find creating sales copy for your product that much easier. I have enjoyed creating this process. I believe it to be valid and I hope your experience is the same.

THE LAW OF ABANDONMENT

- No one wants to be left behind!
- Loneliness is a feeling people want to avoid.
- Fear of Missing Out (FOMO).
- The idea someone else has something they don't can drive them mad.
- How can you associate your product with the emotional trigger of abandonment in your customer?

THE LAW OF ADDICTION

- Once people get a taste of the emotion you provide, they want more.
- Addiction is agnostic – people can get addicted to anything it has to hook them and make them feel temporarily fulfilled, leaving them wanting more.
- With addiction the thing you are offering is not what they want what they want is the feeling that something outside them is going to provide what is missing.
- How can you associate your product with the emotional trigger of addiction in your customer?

THE LAW OF ADVANTAGE

- People want to win. They want stuff. They want stuff other people desire, they want it first, they want it easy.
- They want advantages that are easy to get – makes them feel better and smarter for not having to work for it.
- Primitive feeling – gaining advantage keeps the fear of the dark away – as if they are always pushing back the unknown.
- This is also about achievement – or the sense of achievement that people believe they will get simply by buying your product.
- How can you associate your product with the emotional trigger of advantage in your customer?

THE LAW OF ANTICIPATION

- People love the feeling of being able to secure the future.
- Anticipation gives them something to focus on when the future is unknown.
- Anticipation is a distraction.
- Anticipation is a form of superiority – I have something good coming to me and you don't.
- Anticipation is a form of belonging with like-sorted consumers.
- How can you associate your product with the emotional trigger of anticipation in your customer?

THE LAW OF ANTISOCIAL

- People want to identify with things that other people shun.
- Antisocial is a form of power.
- Antisocial is a thrill in an otherwise boring existence.
- Antisocial imbues being smart in the consumer.
- Antisocial is a reaction to a regimented life.
- How can you associate your product with the emotional trigger of antisocial in your customer?

THE LAW OF ANXIETY

- The feeling that something is wrong, there is a threat and/or they are incapable of taking care of themselves.
- Advertising reminds people of things they can be anxious about and presents solutions, aka "Hurt 'em and heal 'em."
- Exists because people think something "out there" can harm them and therefore the solution also has to come from "out there."
- Anxiety has roots in shame that turns into a poorly configured coping mechanism.
- How can you associate your product with the emotional trigger of anxiety in your customer?

THE LAW OF APPROVAL

- People buy because they want other people to think well of them.
- They want approval from parents, partners and neighbors.
- They want approval from the invisible authority that rules their world.
- They want approval from themselves – that they have worth and they prove it by buying.
- They want the approval that comes from achieving the result you are selling.
- How can you associate your product with the emotional trigger of approval in your customer?

THE LAW OF AUTHORITY

- People crave someone telling them what to do.
- Authority absolves people of responsibility.
- It makes them feel safe.
- Reduces them to a childlike state.
- Make them feel stronger, more important, smarter by association.
- How can you associate your product with the emotional trigger of authority in your customer?

THE LAW OF BEAUTY

- Beauty is a primitive reaction.
- Beauty stirs the desire for perfection.
- Beauty makes people feel better, mood brightener.
- Beauty inspires optimism.
- How can you associate your product with the emotional trigger of beauty in your customer?

THE LAW OF
BEING SMART

- People want to be smart
- They want to acquire goods and services that make them feel smart,
- People want the feeling of being smart by purchase, use and association, it does not mean they want to study or work at being smart.
- People want to be smarter than YOU.
- Being smart is a compensation for other failures.
- How can you associate your product with the emotional trigger of being smart in your customer?

THE LAW OF BIG

- Is your offer so BIG it makes them stop?
- Is it appealing that it makes their imagination take over?
- Does it ignite their greed and make them want to know more?
- How can you associate your product with the emotional trigger of BIG in your customer?

THE LAW OF CARGO CULT SOCIETY

- Cargo cult society is the irrational belief that surrounding yourself with the trappings of success, beauty or wealth automatically confer those qualities.
- It is a form of superstition or magical thinking.
- Give people the opportunity to buy gear, merchandise, branded items so they get that juju.
- Since cargo cult society doesn't work, they will automatically buy more in the hope that one day it will eventually work.
- How can you associate your product with the emotional trigger of cargo cult society in your customer?

THE LAW OF CELEBRITY (TRANSFERENCE)

- People are buying a friendship, approval or love from a celebrity that doesn't know they exist.
- Celebrities induce optimism – they are something I am not.
- This is transference and can happen with or without a celebrity.
- You can transfer your confidence and success to others with marketing.
- People want this transference, they want a transfusion, they want people to wave magic words over their heads and proclaim them worthy.
- You are pulling people forward and they believe it.
- How can you associate your product with the emotional trigger of celebrity (transference) in your customer?

THE LAW OF CERTAINTY

- You have the guaranteed, proven, infallible solution.
- Certainty of outcome requires focus in presentation.
- Often a single result or promise.
- Presented with force, conviction.
- There is no doubt!
- How can you associate your product with the emotional trigger of certainty in your customer?

THE LAW OF CHARITY

- People like the idea of providing for others.
- To crib Ayn Rand it is a form of selfishness or buying virtue.
- They want to be associated with charity and people and organizations that distribute wealth.
- Charity is a form of buying popularity from the customer (you are nice and can therefore be trusted).
- Charity distracts people from the value you are presenting at worst or strengthens it at best.
- Scammers love using charity as a crutch to deflect attention from the intrinsic value of their offer.
- How can you associate your product with the emotional trigger of charity in your customer?

THE LAW OF CONFIDENCE

- People are drawn to confidence. It is a form of power.
- Confidence is a lighthouse or a fort in the wilderness.
- Confidence implies safety.
- People think the confidence projected by the founder, company or product transfers to them.
- How can you associate your product with the emotional trigger of confidence in your customer?

THE LAW OF CONFIRMATION BIAS

- People buy things they already agree with.
- People buy from people they like or already agree with.
- People will buy if you confirm their suspicion.
- People will buy if you show them there is an easier way than has been previously sold to them.
- How can you associate your product with the emotional trigger of confirmation bias in your customer?

THE LAW OF CONFORMITY

- People want to be part of the group
- Conformity is a form of camouflage, "fitting in."
- If they see evidence others are doing it, they will want to do it as well.
- Conforming helps people feel safe.
- Conforming allows people to live on autopilot
- How can you associate your product with the emotional trigger of conformity in your customer?

THE LAW OF CONTROVERSY

- People are attracted to car crashes.
- Controversy allows people to observe conflict without getting hurt.
- Controversy is a means to generate excitement.
- Controversy can be used to attack common enemies.
- Controversy can imply secret knowledge as well as bravery in the face of oppression.
- How can you associate your product with the emotional trigger of controversy in your customer?

THE LAW OF CONVENIENCE

- Is it easy?
- Is it fast?
- Is it simple?
- Has the thinking been removed?
- How can you associate your product with the emotional trigger of convenience in your customer?

THE LAW OF COURAGE

- Courage is necessary for life, yet few have it.
- The product can suggest or confer courage.
- People want to buy what they don't have the strength to do for themselves.
- Buying courage from a leader or movement lets people off the hook for their own shortcomings.
- Courage can be as simple as a personality driven brand or movement – people look up to others who stand up.
- How can you associate your product with the emotional trigger of courage in your customer?

THE LAW OF CROWD EFFECT

- People avoid empty parking lots and restaurants.
- People literally follow a crowd to an unknown destination.
- People's doubts are eased when they see a crowd – despite not seeing any evidence about the product.
- People don't want to be left out.
- People do love a party!
- How can you associate your product with the emotional trigger of crowd effect in your customer?

THE LAW OF CURIOSITY

- This is simple attention getting.
- Something unusual, bright, or loud.
- An intriguing claim that doesn't seem possible but might be.
- Unique, one of a kind, somehow odd but not off-putting.
- Eye-catching.
- How can you associate your product with the emotional trigger of curiosity in your customer?

THE LAW OF DANGER

- People want to avoid danger, even though it gives them a little thrill.
- Advertising reminds them of danger.
- Advertising promises a way to avoid or prevent danger.
- Danger gets people's attention and turns into fear prompting them to be ready to take action.
- How can you associate your product with the emotional trigger of danger in your customer?

THE LAW OF DEFERRAL

- Customers will yield the decision making to an authority or expert
- Customers will pay if you satisfy all their desires and answer all their objections.
- If the authority, expertise pieces are played right, people will roll over and do what you tell them to do.
- People may simply have a lot of choices and just want something expedient.
- How can you associate your product with the emotional trigger of deferral in your customer?

THE LAW OF DEGRADATION

- There is a category of advertising that reinforces people's belief that they don't deserve a good life.
- This is the appeal of drunkenness, antisocial behavior and risk taking.
- This is throwing everything to the wind and not caring about the outcome – though the implication is that it will knock them further down the ladder of life.
- This also indoctrinates the fortunate into self-defeating behavior.
- How can you associate your product with the emotional trigger of degradation in your customer?

THE LAW OF DELIGHT

- People want fun!
- They want to return to a childlike state where everything is nice, safe and uninterrupted enjoyment.
- People want new options, new features.
- They want things to be fresh, refreshed and looking manicured.
- People want to think you exist to serve them.
- How can you associate your product with the emotional trigger of delight in your customer?

THE LAW OF DISTRACTION

- Entertaining your product is likely a distraction from their responsibility.
- Make your distraction more rewarding and less demanding than what they are avoiding.
- Be exciting, intriguing, charismatic.
- Be their friend they want to spend time with, as opposed to the work they are supposed to be doing.
- How can you associate your product with the emotional trigger of distraction in your customer?

THE LAW OF EASY

- Tell them it is easy to get the result.
- They want the result, but they don't want to work.
- Easy is a form of greed and secret knowledge it makes them want it just because it satisfies other triggers such as being smart and laziness.
- How can you associate your product with the emotional trigger of east in your customer?

THE LAW OF EMPTINESS

- People always feel like they are missing out, meaning that something is missing from their lives.
- Advertising and consumption and our products fill that void.
- Advanced advertising is designed to create entire worlds for people to inhabit where they can forget that they have not created meaning for themselves.
- If people weren't plagued by emptiness would they read advertising at all?
- This can be as simple as boredom!
- How can you associate your product with the emotional trigger of emptiness in your customer?

THE LAW OF ENVY

- Envy is juicy. It drives people insane.
- Does not need to be overt – mere images and description of wealth porn make people unbalanced.
- It's not just wanting – it's being mad that you have it and they don't.
- Is used to convince people to make unwise choices.
- Having an advantage induces envy, success induces envy.
- Big part of envy is that it is perceived as unfair.
- How can you associate your product with the emotional trigger of envy in your customer?

THE LAW OF EXCITEMENT

- Dah dat datta dat da! It's a parade!
- This is the loud salesman the flashing lights the fireworks.
- The presentation is where most of this resides – things aren't exciting. It's the idea of the thing.
- Gotta get a Dell dude is the daddy of all this on YouTube.
- Often tied to scams, schemes, theft, fraud. And theft is exciting. It's free stuff.
- How can you associate your product with the emotional trigger of excitement in your customer?

THE LAW OF EXCLUSION

- The neglected flip side of insider status
- When they have it they are part of the group, but the most important thing is who is excluded. And people love it.
- Infers superiority or chosen status.
- Often practical as in country clubs, professional associations, and certain memberships, where you know the non-special people are not allowed.
- How can you associate your product with the emotional trigger of exclusion in your customer?

THE LAW OF EXPERTISE

- People want to buy expertise because it is practical to trade dollars for years of knowledge and capability.
- Buying expertise is a status item.
- Expertise conveys confidence and trust, a guarantee.
- People want to be aligned with experts for superstitious reasons.
- People think that some of the expert status transfers to them at the point of sale, also a superstitious belief.
- How can you associate your product with the emotional trigger of expertise in your customer?

THE LAW OF FAITH

- People want to believe.
- Elaborate and perhaps sincere promises made directly to the customer's sense of fair play or moral value.
- Basic consumer trust.
- An appeal made to the customer to believe in a mission greater than mere business.
- How can you associate your product with the emotional trigger of faith in your customer?

THE LAW OF FANTASY

- Humans naturally daydream, offer them a magic carpet ride.
- Fantasizing is free, it is enjoyable and risk-free.
- What fantasy does buying your product deliver to your customer – a new way of life? Status? Wealth?
- This is painting a picture, demonstrating wealth, acting confident, promising that they too can live the fantasy life of their dreams.
- People engage in multiple fantasies every day. This may be more important than figuring out their problems – what you want is the fantasy solution they already have in mind for their problem.
- How can you associate your product with the emotional trigger of fantasy in your customer?

THE LAW OF FEAR

- Human beings are afraid of the dark. This is the driver responsible for civilization and war.
- There is plenty to be afraid of. Advertisers harness fear to get people's attention and offer a solution for just one item in their fear inventory.
- Customers have more than one fear – your product may solve one of them, but you can extend the solution to solving many other fears, a domino effect.
- Fear makes people compliant.
- How can you associate your product with the emotional trigger of fear in your customer?

THE LAW OF FREE

- Free stuff is against the laws of nature. Everyone still wants free stuff.
- It is a form of cheating, of gaming the system, breaking the rules.
- Free gets people's attention.
- Will always attract non-customers.
- It is a bribe to a dishonest person, so you have been warned.
- The best kind of free requires some form of reciprocity.
- How can you associate your product with the emotional trigger of free in your customer?

THE LAW OF FREEDOM

- People say they want freedom - but work, pressure, obligation. It is a form of fantasy. Advertising satisfies this need and then they don't do anything.
- How can you associate your product with the emotional trigger of freedom in your customer?

THE LAW OF FRUSTRATION

- Stuff doesn't work out the way we planned.
- Life is full of daily frustrations.
- A small delight, a solution to a problem, a diversion for a minute is welcomed by customers.
- People feel no one cares about their frustration – show you care about your customers'.
- How can you associate your product with the emotional trigger of frustration in your customer?

THE LAW OF FULFILLMENT

- Related to emptiness – fulfillment temporarily eases the customer's pain.
- Helps people solve something they felt was missing.
- Can be something they can brag about or show off.
- Satisfies a trope they had such as graduating from college or getting professional certification.
- Enables leisure or ease.
- Fulfillment can also mean the fulfillment of a promise made to the customer.
- How can you associate your product with the emotional trigger of fulfillment in your customer?

THE LAW OF FUTURE

- Another form of fantasy - people often don't create their future so they allow advertisers to paint one for them.
- This is a deep trigger that gets them emotionally committed to your product – because without your product they have no future.
- How can you associate your product with the emotional trigger of the future in your customer?

THE LAW OF GREED

- The universal desire to acquire. To have something for themselves, to have something others don't.
- Signals a deep fear and a drive to achieve safety.
- Can destabilize people's critical thinking, cause them to let their guard down.
- Something everyone agrees on.
- A roomful of greedy people working to achieve a financial goal is like an orgy.
- Greed is often something big, seen as unattainable but you have the key which adds value to your offer.
- How can you associate your product with the emotional trigger of greed in your customer?

THE LAW OF GROWTH

- Growth is an esoteric goal people say they want because they are in an obedient mindset.
- It is for the aimless, the unsatisfied, therefore easy to sell but tough to assign a value since its benefit is not always monetary.
- Can be related to associated goals – such as in fitness where you grow in confidence and are then able to achieve other goals such as money and professional advancement.
- How can you associate your product with the emotional trigger of growth in your customer?

THE LAW OF GUILT

- What has your customer done or failed to do?
- Have they failed to achieve something or provide for themselves or family.
- Have they neglected a responsibility, such as having life insurance which is a guilt sale.
- Have they lacked courage or given up?
- How can you associate your product with the emotional trigger of guilt in your customer?

THE LAW OF HERO WORSHIP

- People throw themselves at the famous, the attractive, the powerful and the confident.
- This is about the product or founder as a leader worth following.
- Hero worship implies they can be a hero to others if they buy the product and obtain its benefits. Could be summer camp, a minivan, advanced degree or being in a helping profession.
- People want to be heroic, yet they are looking to others to provide it to them. This is contradictory which is why it works. The people who want to be heroes but can't, need heroes.
- How can you associate your product with the emotional trigger of hero worship in your customer?

THE LAW OF HOARDING

- People buy more than they need for psychological reasons.
- Hoarders are repeat customers!
- Hoarders don't use the products they buy.
- Harding is an addiction.
- Hoarding responds to new, the latest, upgrades, even more benefits, etc. Give them more reasons to buy more of the stuff they never use.
- How can you associate your product with the emotional trigger of hoarding in your customer?

THE LAW OF HOPE

- The universal marketing trigger.
- People are in their lives, when a message comes along it must give them hope that will relieve their current concern.
- As such, hope is a distraction, a pretty bauble or birdsong.
- Besides being a distraction it must be brighter, better, happier than where they are now.
- How can you associate your product with the emotional trigger of hope in your customer?

THE LAW OF IDENTITY

- People buy what they are.
- Purchases confirm identity and strengthen it.
- People also buy what they want to be.
- Because people are driven by identity, obtaining goods and services becomes intertwined with their goals and even the way they pursue them.
- Bumper stickers, vanity plates, designer handbags, etc.
- Advertisers present goods as "someone you want to be."
- How can you associate your product with the emotional trigger of identity in your customer?

THE LAW OF IMMORTALITY

- This in in the back of everyone's mind, though no one likes to talk about it
- But advertisers need to know about it because it drives behavior.
- Explains part of the drive behind cosmetic surgery as well as wealth and conspicuous consumption.
- Effective for legacy type advertising, achievement orientation.
- People want to stave off the inevitable.
- You can distract people from it, you can promise them riches and fame, you can assure them they will be larger than life.
- How can you associate your product with the emotional trigger of immortality in your customer?

THE LAW OF INADEQUACY

- No one feels they are good enough.
- Our job is to remind them!
- But you can be good enough if you buy this, do that or drink this.
- It's diabolical.
- How can you associate your product with the emotional trigger of inadequacy in your customer?

THE LAW OF
INSIDER STATUS

- If you are inside, you are better than the person who is outside.
- Basic sorting mechanism and everyone is keeping score.
- Insider status makes people feel powerful.
- It confers authority and confidence.
- They obtain it by buying, by joining by learning the thing that others don't have or know. (TED Talks!)
- It is often simply the cost of entry – then to remain an insider you have to do this, this and this.
- How can you associate your product with the emotional trigger of insider status in your customer?

THE LAW OF INTRIGUE

- Well this is new, and unusual and mysterious.
- Often the founder presenting themselves as the holder of great knowledge.
- Presented as secret or new discovery or limited edition.
- Guarded behind closed doors, velvet rope.
- How can you associate your product with the emotional trigger of intrigue in your customer?

THE LAW OF JEALOUSY

- People are always comparing themselves to others.
- Advertisers ride the clutch – look at them who have this.
- You can have it – if you have the money, if you are smart enough, if you have the courage, etc.
- Another trigger that causes irrational behavior.
- How can you associate your product with the emotional trigger of jealousy in your customer?

THE LAW OF LAZINESS

- No one wants to work or expend any effort to get anything they want – which is everything.
- Being able to be lazy is a perverse indicator that you are smart.
- People want convenience, they want it easy, they want it now and they want you to kiss their ass.
- Laziness is a form of revenge!
- How can you associate your product with the emotional trigger of laziness in your customer?

THE LAW OF LONELINESS

- Everyone is looking for connection.
- People identify and get a false sense of community with their purchases.
- Advertising is a form of babysitting or companionship (late night infomercials?)
- People buy to belong, to feel less lonely, to be part of a group where they may meet or have kinship with other.
- How can you associate your product with the emotional trigger of loneliness in your customer?

THE LAW OF LOSS

- People will do more to avoid loss than acquire gain.
- The idea of loss, like abandonment or loneliness, is primitive.
- Demonstrate what they will miss by not buying.
- Demonstrate what other people are enjoying by buying.
- Demonstrate how other people joined the party after hesitating.
- How can you associate your product with the emotional trigger of loss in your customer?

THE LAW OF LUST

- Can be pure sex. Either the actual product or imagery used to get people's attention.
- A form of powerlessness looking to gain power.
- Similar to greed but dirtier, more primal.
- Wanting driven by unsatisfied desires or simply unhinged acquisitiveness.
- How can you associate your product with the emotional trigger of lust in your customer?

THE LAW OF MAGIC

- The essence of advertising – words and pictures can make your dreams come true? Really?
- People are primitive and believe in magical transformation from one state to another with no effort or visible mechanism.
- Magic is a transportation mechanism – from attention to fantasy to action.
- People want it to be true.
- Usually involves some small or ceremonial sacrifice, i.e., if you send in $10 now you will have the life of your dreams.
- Magic does keep people going in life. It alleviates struggle.
- How can you associate your product with the emotional trigger of magic in your customer?

THE LAW OF MECHANISM

- Demonstrate how it works. The Hula-hoop is fun, watch this video of squealing kids and adults.
- Explain how it works – pictures, animation, drawings.
- Provide proof that the mechanism is repeatable.
- How can you associate your product with the emotional trigger of mechanism in your customer?

THE LAW OF MOTIVATION

- Are you really motivating people? Or manipulating them?
- Your presence is motivational – people who take a risk are "a light in the darkness."
- Your words and images of a better tomorrow are motivation – which is hope transformed into action.
- Motivation is encouragement to do hard things without making it look that hard, "I'll be with you every step of the way."
- Motivation emphasizes the result of the hard work, makes it look like a party.
- How can you associate your product with the emotional trigger of motivation in your customer?

THE LAW OF NARRATIVE

- People have a narrative in their head.
- You are presenting a narrative.
- You want to join the two together, so they enlist in yours.
- Narrative is a woven continuity story which helps people make sense of existence.
- Narrative doesn't actually exist. It is a human invention, i.e., the story of creation.
- How can you associate your product with the emotional trigger of narrative in your customer?

THE LAW OF NEW

- Is it new?
- New implies a breakthrough, a new advance and secret knowledge.
- New is a greed multiplier – if it is new then no one else knows about it and it has a built-in advantage.
- New also triggers their desire to be satisfied, they want to be first to be smart to be an insider and to have an edge.
- How can you associate your product with the emotional trigger of new in your customer?

THE LAW OF NORMALCY

- People buy what they think is normal or should be.
- A form of conformity.
- Normalcy is aspirational – they want life to be orderly.
- Advertisers have to make things appear normal – historically, this was true with both orange juice and toothpaste.
- How can you associate your product with the emotional trigger of normalcy in your customer?

THE LAW OF NOSTALGIA

- The way things used to be.
- An appeal to the past that may not have existed and may in fact have just been advertising from a previous era.
- Psychological safety blanket.
- An appeal for order and harmony.
- How can you associate your product with the emotional trigger of nostalgia in your customer?

THE LAW OF NOVELTY

- Is it new?
- Is it different?
- Is it unique?
- Does it arouse curiosity?
- Are other people talking about it?
- This is a form of delight and curiosity.
- How can you associate your product with the emotional trigger of novelty in your customer?

THE LAW OF OBEDIENCE

- "Give me what I want, and I'll go away."
- Do what I say. Authoritarian posture.
- People obey the authority of someone talking to them impersonally through a screen.
- Ultimately all purchases are acts of obedience.
- How can you associate your product with the emotional trigger of obedience in your customer?

THE LAW OF OBLIGATION

- You owe me, the world owes me.
- Reminding the customer they have an obligation to do certain things, and to certain people – or to society.
- You are giving them a way to fulfill their obligation – 1-800-FLOWERS, LOL.
- It is coercion, presented as a warm and fluffy story.
- Reminding people of their responsibilities.
- How can you associate your product with the emotional trigger of obligation in your customer?

THE LAW OF OPTIMISM

- You are presenting the miracle antidote to a world of darkness and despair, and I am not kidding.
- People consume a diet of bad news and stress every day.
- You are telling people it is going to be okay.
- You are reassuring them and they will repay this kindness with sales.
- How can you associate your product with the emotional trigger of obligation in your customer?

THE LAW OF PANIC

- Similar to danger, but more immediate.
- Pandemic, anyone?
- Hoarding, guns, safes, doorbell cameras?
- Linked to scarcity, getting into Ivy League school, competitive situations, sports, social drama.
- People will act (buy) when they are panicked.
- How can you associate your product with the emotional trigger of panic in your customer?

THE LAW OF PARANOIA

- Everyone thinks they are being watched, because they are.
- People are afraid of what might happen.
- They want to protect themselves.
- They want to prevent disasters.
- Paranoia can be healthy, i.e., hurricane insurance.
- How can you associate your product with the emotional trigger of paranoia in your customer?

THE LAW OF PERMISSION

- People need an authority to tell them it's okay to do, be or have what they really want.
- Your product may be no more than a vehicle to give someone permission.
- Permission implies hesitation, so advertisers must soothe that fear.
- Permission is about showing the world is a big place with lots of options and opportunities; it is based on optimism.
- How can you associate your product with the emotional trigger of permission in your customer?

THE LAW OF POSSIBILITY

- Anything is possible!
- More to the point, anything is possible for YOU! (I mean, look at her, she did it.)
- Again, optimism, energy, and motivation.
- All you need is the widget I have right here – your life can be bigger, brighter, happier and most important the envy of others.
- How can you associate your product with the emotional trigger of possibility in your customer?

THE LAW OF POWER

- People crave power but don't have the courage to reach for it (or even admit it.)
- Advertising is a display of power, which makes people feel weak for seeing what they have not got.
- People believe there will be a magical transfer of power when they buy.
- People gravitate to power; they worship it, and they will fight for it just not in open combat. They will beg, negotiate and maneuver their way to power, which is the opposite (not rational).
- Exude power. In your person and in your product. In your knowledge, in your expertise, in your results and in your conviction that you have the solution to their problem.
- How can you associate your product with the emotional trigger of power in your customer?

THE LAW OF PRIDE

- Pride will motivate people to lose weight, get an education or work harder – they don't want to break the belief they have in themselves.
- Pride, as a form of power in the advertiser, will cause people to gravitate to you.
- People want to be able to hold their head up and look others in the eye.
- Advertisers remind people they have not reached their full potential, causing shame that has to be rectified with pride.
- How can you associate your product with the emotional trigger of pride in your customer?

THE LAW OF PROOF

- This is scientific studies, data, mathematical equations.
- Testimonials are a classic form of proof.
- Demonstration is also a form of proof
- Can be associated with ancient secrets that have worked for thousands of years.
- Proof builds trust and desire.
- How can you associate your product with the emotional trigger of proof in your customer?

THE LAW OF PUBLICITY

- When people are talking about you, you must be important right?
- Social media is publicity, driven by the product owner (influencer)
- It is the getting of attention.
- Better yet it is getting other people to talk about you, mention you or criticize you – it extends your reach beyond your own efforts.
- When it comes from someone else, it enhances your credibility.
- "Force multiplier"
- How can you associate your product with the emotional trigger of publicity in your customer?

THE LAW OF RECOGNITION

- My God, people crave recognition.
- They want people to think well of them to say there are smart to admire them and quite frankly to kiss their ass.
- They want to be told they are special.
- They want membership cards, plaques and minivan magnets.
- Recognition is a way to reinforce their identity.
- Look ma, I made it!
- How can you associate your product with the emotional trigger of recognition in your customer?

THE LAW OF REDEMPTION

- I coulda' been a contender!
- People want a second chance.
- They want to be told it's not their fault, they got cheated and if they get one more shot, this time they will make something of themselves.
- People want a mechanism to overcome guilt and shame.
- Redemption is their secret prayer!
- How can you associate your product with the emotional trigger of redemption in your customer?

THE LAW OF REGRET

- Everyone has regrets, the advertiser's job is to make them feel bad about it – bad enough to buy my shit.
- Helping people avoid regret by pointing out examples may be a public service!
- All is forgiven, and since you don't want it to happen again, buy this.
- Addressing regrets gets people's attention – it is a sore topic.
- Addressing regrets encourages compliance.
- How can you associate your product with the emotional trigger of regret in your customer?

THE LAW OF REMEDY FOR DISCOURAGEMENT

- The remedy for discouragement may be direct – you need a coach to avoid failing again.
- The remedy for discouragement may be indirect – here's a quart of ice cream and a spoon. Don't bother with the bowl you deserve it, you had a hard day.
- The existence of advertising is often the remedy and people will stop to consider it – how do you get them to buy the remedy?
- If someone is beaten up by a literal failure they do need encouragement.
- How can you associate your product with the emotional trigger of remedy for discouragement in your customer?

THE LAW OF RESOLUTION

- What's the point of your long-winded narrative?
- Provide a picture of what the end state looks like.
- Resolution involves a change of emotional state from perturbed to harmony.
- Imply or demonstrate you have the answer to all their concerns.
- How can you associate your product with the emotional trigger of resolution in your customer?

THE LAW OF REVENGE

- No one likes to talk about this one, but it is huge.
- People want revenge – for being left out, for being ridiculed, for losing, for being short or ugly or fat – THEY WANT REVENGE!
- They love it when someone else is harmed or suffers.
- Revenge in advertising is usually a proxy to help the customer relieve an emotional wound.
- How can you associate your product with the emotional trigger of revenge in your customer?

THE LAW OF SAFE

- Is it low risk?
- Is it easy to do, low cost and does it work?
- Is it foolproof and injury proof?
- Does it help them get a big and awesome result without endangering their comfort?
- How can you associate your product with the emotional trigger of safe in your customer?

THE LAW OF SATISFACTION

- Can you put a smile on their face?
- Can you delight them for a moment?
- Can you deliver competence?
- Can you listen to and understand their needs?
- How can you associate your product with the emotional trigger of satisfaction in your customer?

THE LAW OF SCARCITY

- Don't delay, act now, supplies are running out!
- Scarcity increases value.
- Scarcity provokes immediate action.
- Failing to respond to scarcity makes people feel stupid.
- How can you associate your product with the emotional trigger of scarcity in your customer?

THE LAW OF SECRET KNOWLEDGE

- There is a psychological need to pay for secret knowledge – in the customer's mind paying for it creates a false impression that they have absorbed the knowledge and are now an expert.
- Secret knowledge implies discovery, above average intelligence and access to smart people who are keepers of secrets.
- Secret knowledge reinforces the idea that the world is an unfair place – buying secret knowledge evens the score.
- Legitimate secret knowledge is a force multiplier for the customer – for a few dollars they get to buy 10 or 20 years of expertise.
- This is the realm of new discovery! Breakthrough process!
- How can you associate your product with the emotional trigger of secret knowledge in your customer?

THE LAW OF SELF-DOUBT

- Plagued by self-doubt – Extraterrestrial report on the state of the human race.
- Your job is to remind them of the self-doubt and then cure it – because now their self-doubt is evident and a source of shame and must be remedied.
- You must be aware of the customer's self-doubt and assure them they can do it – remember the "For Dummies" book series?
- Self-doubt is persistent so everything you do must be designed to keep it at bay.
- How can you associate your product with the emotional trigger of self-doubt in your customer?

THE LAW OF SHAME

- People's failings are with them at all moments.
- Tell them it's okay.
- Give them a means to remedy the shame.
- Shame haunts people.
- Go lightly.
- How can you associate your product with the emotional trigger of shame in your customer?

THE LAW OF SPECTACLE

- Fireworks!
- This is the big show, the World Wrestling Federation, the bombastic announcer.
- Spectacle allows people to forget themselves and surrender to the mob, which means all self-control which means their wallets.
- This is showmanship.
- How can you associate your product with the emotional trigger of spectacle in your customer?

THE LAW OF STATUS

- People crave status – meaning they want other people to know how important, rich, good-looking or smart they are.
- Status can be direct or indirect – either the purchase gives them status or enables them to get status.
- Status implies scarcity and expense.
- Status is also power, at least perceived.
- How can you associate your product with the emotional trigger of status in your customer?

THE LAW OF STICKING IT TO THE MAN

- This is one of the main drivers of get rich programs.
- This is a revenge play – if the customer feels cheated or locked out of opportunity, they want the reward of the offer as well as the feeling of "they showed them."
- Sticking it to the man is anti-social, defiant.
- Sticking it to the man creates a community of like-minded people.
- Sticking it to the man implies there are secrets to success and happiness that have been withheld.
- How can you associate your product with the emotional trigger of sticking it to the man in your customer?

THE LAW OF SUPERIORITY

- I am better than you.
- This is weaponized status.
- This is a power play – buying status or achievement in order to lord it over others.
- The person who needs to feel superior can be conned.
- True superiority is earned and won – this can be used for niche products that promote hard work.
- How can you associate your product with the emotional trigger of superiority in your customer?

THE LAW OF SUPERSTITION

- People believe in things that are not real.
- They pray, consult astrologers and believe there are invisible forces that both hinder and help them.
- You, the advertiser, are the invisible force!
- Superstitious people never stop believing.
- How can you associate your product with the emotional trigger of superiority in your customer?

THE LAW OF SUSPICION

- You can confirm people's suspicions with your breakthrough secret – there has to be an easier way!
- You must allay people's suspicions of you – you can do this directly, as in, you may be asking yourself who is this guy?
- You can help alleviate people's suspicions of the world, of danger, by offering them a solution geared to peace of mind.
- You should acknowledge that people have good reason to be suspicious.
- How can you associate your product with the emotional trigger of suspicion in your customer?

THE LAW OF
THE ENEMY

- The enemy focuses the mind, creating fear and danger.
- The enemy is a rally point to oppose.
- The enemy is also someone to blame.
- The enemy can be defeated with the purchase of this product.
- How can you associate your product with the emotional trigger of the enemy in your customer?

THE LAW OF TRUST

- There is an automatic amount of trust – until you lie.
- Demonstration and proof builds trust.
- Expertise builds trust.
- Customer service builds trust.
- Testimonials build trust.
- How can you associate your product with the emotional trigger of trust in your customer?

THE LAW OF URGENCY

- Do it now!
- Deadlines and scarcity.
- How much longer do you want to be a loser?
- If you don't do it today, tomorrow is going to look the same.
- People are lazy and procrastinate, urgency moves your ask to the top of their imaginary list.
- How can you associate your product with the emotional trigger of urgency in your customer?

THE LAW OF VALIDATION

- Simple thank you for your order validates the customer's existence – and faith in you.
- Your argument validates their suspicion.
- Validation puts them at ease.
- Validation is a way for the customer to confirm their identity, so they are buying their emotional triggers which are actually their identity triggers.
- How can you associate your product with the emotional trigger of validation in your customer?

THE LAW OF VALUE

- People want to feel it was a fair exchange.
- They DO NOT want to get cheated.
- Quality is part of value – the feeling their purchase affirms their choice, their wisdom and again, their identity.
- People will brag about value, encouraging word of mouth advertising.
- Value is also about BOGO, discounts and explained value, as in 20 years of experience in this program for only $299.
- How can you associate your product with the emotional trigger of value in your customer?

THE LAW OF VANITY

- Vain people need to constantly be reassured that they are beautiful, successful, or rich.
- Vanity is fear of death!
- Vanity is a weakness marketers exploit.
- Vanity is insatiable.
- How can you associate your product with the emotional trigger of vanity in your customer?

THE LAW OF VICTORY

- "People want some of that victory."
- Victory is an intoxicant. It makes us feel safe and powerful.
- Demonstrate your victory.
- Tell them they can do it – especially if they associate with you.
- How can you associ ate your product with the emotional trigger of victory in your customer?

THE LAW OF VIOLENCE

- Violent imagery is a dark trigger but that does not make it invalid.
- Violence is about one person exerting their will over another.
- People are attracted to violence – how do all those videos get on the internet – 2 guys fighting, 20 people filming.
- Violence in advertising is about danger, self-preservation or winning over outsider groups.
- How can you associate your product with the emotional trigger of violence in your customer?

THE LAW OF VITALITY

- Life attracts life.
- People are superstitious, the more life they collect the more they think they have.
- Vitality is about motion, growth and renewal.
- You must demonstrate vitality.
- You must promise vitality.
- How can you associate your product with the emotional trigger of vitality in your customer?